CERT Animal Response I - Instructor Guide

978-1718619029

CERT ANIMAL RESPONSE I

In this module, you will learn about:

- **Animal Issues in Emergency Management:** Why animal response is an essential component of emergency preparedness

- **Animal-Related Emergency Management Functions:** Emergency management functions that require handling, containing, or managing animals

- **Disaster Planning for Your Animals:** How to prepare a disaster kit and disaster plan for your own animals

- **General Animal Behavior:** Behavior patterns of predator and prey animals, domesticated animals, and specific species, including wild and exotic animals

- **Preview of *CERT Animal Response II*:** Introduction to the *CERT Animal Response II* module.

TABLE OF CONTENTS

PAGE

OBJECTIVES	At the conclusion of this module, the participants will be able to:

- Explain why animal issues are an important consideration in emergency management
- Demonstrate knowledge of animal-related emergency management functions
- Explain how to prepare their own animals for an emergency
- Describe general guidelines for handling animals

SCOPE

The topics that will be discussed in this module are:

- Animal Issues in Emergency Management
- Animal-Related Emergency Management Functions
- Disaster Planning for Your Animals
- General Animal Behavior
- Preview of *CERT Animal Response II*

ESTIMATED COMPLETION TIME

3 hours

TRAINING METHODS

The lead instructor will begin by welcoming the participants to the training, introducing him- or herself and the other instructor(s), and making any necessary administrative announcements.

The instructor will begin an activity to introduce the participants to each other and illustrate the range of topics that are important in the management of animals during disasters. During this activity, each participant will introduce him- or herself and provide a brief description of why he or she is attending the training.

Next, the instructor will briefly explain the module purpose and training objectives and discuss the topics that will be covered in the session.

The instructor will then lead a group discussion by asking participants why they think animal issues are an important component of emergency management. The instructor will conclude the discussion by asserting that animals are an essential consideration in disaster preparedness and emergency response.

**TRAINING METHODS
CONTINUED**

Next, the instructor will lead a group discussion by asking participants to identify animal-related emergency management functions. The instructor will provide examples and additional information throughout the discussion. The purpose of the discussion is for the class to consider the wide range of emergency functions that may include animal encounters.

The instructor will then begin a lecture on preparing animals for disaster. The instructor will provide information from FEMA's disaster plans and emergency supply checklists for pets and livestock and present a video from the FEMA Web site. The instructor will ask participants to use the information just learned to outline a disaster plan for their own animal(s) or animals with which they are familiar. The instructor will ask a few volunteers to share their plans with the class.

Next, the instructor will present photos of animals with similar characteristics and ask participants to identify the commonalities between the animals. The instructor will review the differences between predator and prey animals and explain issues concerning animal domestication.

The instructor will then divide the class into two teams and conduct a game so that participants can share their knowledge of cat and dog behavior. After the game, the instructor will test participants' knowledge by displaying several animal photos and asking the class to identify the behavior of each animal.

The instructor will conclude the training with a summary of the information discussed throughout the module and a brief scenario introducing some of the content that will be learned in the next module, *CERT Animal Response II*.

The instructor is encouraged to add pertinent information to this Instructor Guide but should never subtract material.

RESOURCES REQUIRED

- *CERT Animal Response I* Instructor Guide
- *CERT Animal Response I* Participant Manual
- *CERT Animal Response I* PowerPoint slides
- FEMA video, "Animals in Emergencies for Owners"

  This 35-minute video is intended to help pet and livestock owners prepare to protect their animals during emergencies. The video can be viewed or downloaded at: http://emc.ornl.gov/training/animals-in-emergencies/animals-in-emergencies.html.

EQUIPMENT

The following equipment is required for this module:

- A computer with PowerPoint software and Windows Media Player
- A computer projector and screen
- A large easel pad and three black markers
- Blank, lined paper
- Two bells
- Candy or animal crackers

PREPARATION

Review this module and add local information wherever requested. Prepare information on:

- State and local laws that affect the emergency management of animals
- Details of the local jurisdiction's Emergency Operations Plan (EOP) that addresses animal issues
- Disasters that are likely to occur in your area
- Animals that are common in your area, including local wildlife and farm animals
- Large animal populations in your community, such as those at livestock farms, kennels, zoos, pet stores, breeding facilities, etc.

NOTES

A suggested time plan for this module is as follows:

Welcome and Introductions .... 10 minutes

Animal Issues in Emergency Management..................... 20 minutes

Animal-Related Emergency Management Functions ...... 20 minutes

Disaster Planning for Your Animals .... 60 minutes

General Animal Behavior .... 60 minutes

Preview of *CERT Animal Response II* .... 5 minutes

Module Summary and Closing .... 5 minutes

Total Time: 3 hours

PARTICIPANT PREREQUISITES

Participants must have completed the *CERT Basic Training* course.

INSTRUCTOR QUALIFICATIONS

Instructors for *CERT Animal Response I* should have the following qualifications:

- Completion of *CERT Basic Training* course

- Knowledge of the local EOP

- Trainer experience

- Professional experience in emergency response *and* animal response, animal control, veterinary medicine, or other animal services

ACKNOWLEDGEMENTS

The National CERT Program would like to thank the following people who participated in a focus group to develop this training module:

Nancy Barr, DVM
Senior Field Veterinarian
Michigan Department of Agriculture

Robert Beckmann, Jr.
CERT Program Director
Nassau County, NY

Penny Burke
Program Specialist
Community Preparedness Division, FEMA

Anne Culver
Disaster Training Consultant
The Humane Society of the United States

Kevin Dennison, DVM
Western Regional Emergency Programs Manager
USDA APHIS Animal Care

Naomi Flam
CERT Program Instructor
Fresno, CA

Charlie O'Brien
Code Compliance Officer
Richfield, MN; Public Safety

Lt. John Reynolds
Maricopa County Animal Care and Control
Phoenix, AZ

SOURCES

- The Humane Society of the United States Disaster Animal Response Training *Personal Planning* Instructor Guide
- The Humane Society of the United States Disaster Animal Response Training *Animal Facility Planning* Instructor Guide
- The Humane Society of the United States Disaster Animal Response Training *Small Animal Behavior* Instructor Guide
- The Humane Society of the United States Disaster Animal Response Training *Exotic Animal Handling* Instructor Guide
- The Humane Society of the United States Disaster Animal Response Training *Large Animal Handling* Instructor Guide
- The Humane Society of the United States Disaster Animal Response Training *Animal First Aid* Instructor Guide
- Colorado Veterinary Medical Foundation Community Animal Response Training *Consolidated Units 1-5* Instructor Guide
- Colorado Veterinary Medical Foundation Community Animal Response Training *Unit 6 Animal Handling* Instructor Guide
- Federal Emergency Management Agency (FEMA) *Information for Pet Owners* and *Information for Livestock Owners*

Notes

Notes

INSTRUCTOR GUIDANCE	CONTENT
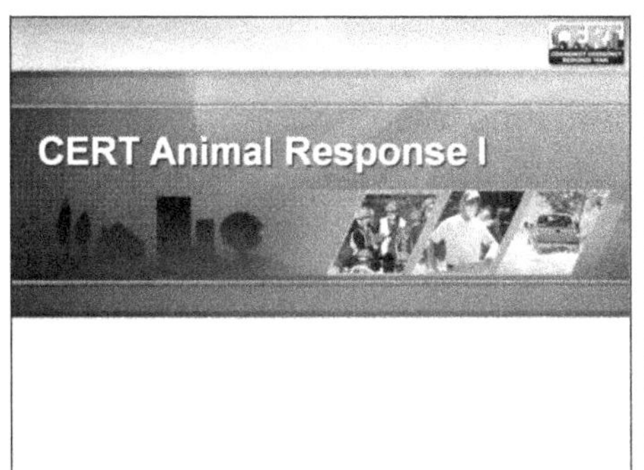**Display Slide 0**	## *Welcome and Introductions* Welcome the participants to the CERT Animal Response I supplemental training. Introduce yourselves and provide some background information about your past experiences in emergency response and animal issues. ### Introductions Develop a class roster by passing around a sheet of paper to have the participants write down their contact information or check in on a roster created from registration information. If time allows and participants do not already know each other, have them introduce themselves by giving their names and the reason they want to learn more about animal response. ### Administrative Announcements Make any necessary announcements such as: ■ Schedule of breaks for this session ■ Emergency exits ■ Restroom locations, smoking policy, etc. ■ Module completion requirements

INSTRUCTOR GUIDANCE	CONTENT

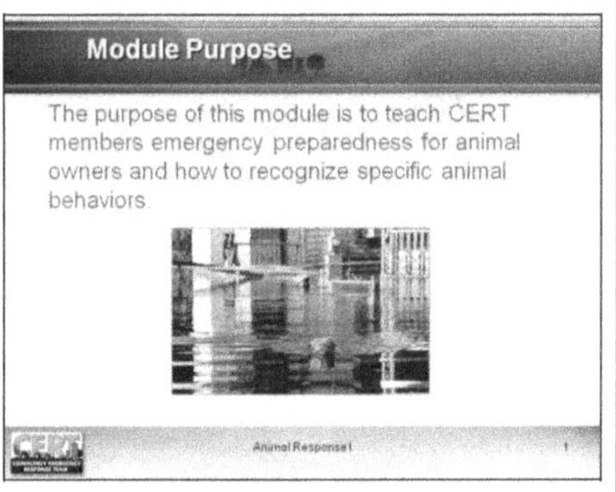

Display Slide 1

If there are CARTs, SARTs, or DARTs in your community, be prepared to provide contact information to the group.

Module Purpose

Explain that this module is the first of two modules that make up the CERT Animal Response training. Introduce the purpose of this module, CERT Animal Response I.

The purpose of this module is to teach CERT members emergency preparedness for animal owners and how to recognize specific animal behaviors.

Explain that the CERT supplemental training on animals is meant to support the disaster response training that participants have already received in the CERT Basic Training course. In terms of disaster response, the focus of this module and CERT Animal Response II will be preparation for situations involving animals that they may encounter in performing their broader CERT response functions.

Note that this is different from training for volunteer response teams such as County or Community Animal Response Teams (CARTs), State Animal Response Teams (SARTs), or Disaster Animal Response Teams (DARTs). The mission of these types of teams is specifically animal response and rescue during disasters.

Caution participants that this training is insufficient to make them competent professional animal handlers.

INSTRUCTOR GUIDANCE	CONTENT

Display Slide 2

Animal Categories

Finally, explain that the material in this module and *CERT Animal Response II* is intended to generally cover six categories of animals:

- Household pets, domesticated animals such as a dog, cat, bird, rabbit, rodent, or turtle that is kept in the home for pleasure rather than commercial purposes

- Service animals, trained to assist people with disabilities, etc.

- For-profit animals, including livestock and commercial animals such as those bred and/or trained for sale or other profit

- Non-commercial livestock such as horses kept for personal recreation

- Wildlife, those wild animals indigenous to an area

- Exotic animals, which may be pets

Note that service animals are a category defined by the Americans with Disabilities Act (ADA) and that they require special consideration by emergency responders.

- A service animal is any animal that is individually trained to provide assistance to a person with a disability.

- Most people are familiar with dogs that guide people who are blind or have low vision, but there are many other functions that service animals perform for people with a variety of disabilities. Examples include:

  - Alerting people who are deaf or hard of hearing to sounds

  - Pulling wheelchairs; carrying or retrieving items for people with mobility disabilities or limited use of arms or hands

  - Assisting people with disabilities to maintain their balance or stability

INSTRUCTOR GUIDANCE	CONTENT
	• Alerting people to and protecting them during medical events such as seizures

Explain that service animals may require certain considerations:

- During emergencies many emergency shelters do not allow residents or volunteers to bring their pets or other animals inside, but shelters must make exceptions to allow people with disabilities to be accompanied by their service animals.

- Service animals must be provided with essential services at human shelters.

- Be careful to avoid touching or speaking to any service animal while it is working.

Note that considerations specific to each of the other categories of animals are identified in the material.

What You Will Learn

List the topics that will be learned in the module:

- Animal Issues in Emergency Management

- Animal-Related Emergency Management Functions

- Disaster Planning for Your Animals

- General Animal Behavior

- Preview of *CERT Animal Response II*

Display Slide 3

INSTRUCTOR GUIDANCE	CONTENT
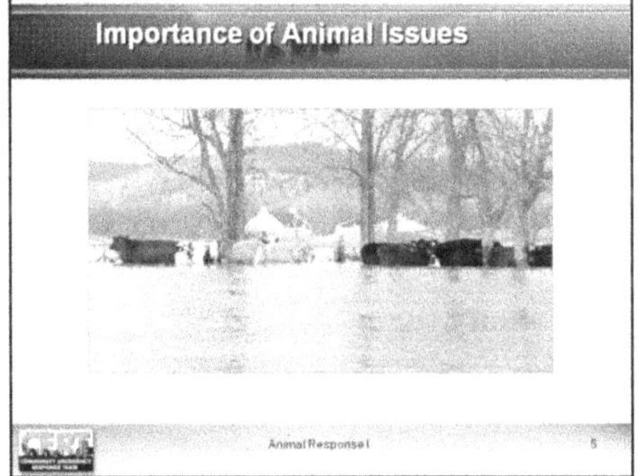 **Display Slide 4**	**Module Objectives** At the end of this module, participants will be able to: - Explain why animal issues are an important consideration in emergency management - Demonstrate knowledge of animal-related emergency management functions - Explain emergency preparedness for animal owners - Describe general guidelines for handling animals

Display Slide 4

Display Slide 5

Record responses on an easel pad or white board. Suggested responses:

- Public safety
- Federal law and policy
- Public health
- Economic impact
- Environmental concerns
- Safety of first responders

Animal Issues in Emergency Management

Introduce the next topic, "Animal Issues in Emergency Management."

Importance of Animal Issues

Why are animals an important component of disaster response?

INSTRUCTOR GUIDANCE	CONTENT

	Cover the following information on why animals are an important component of disaster response if it was not already covered in the class discussion.
	
	 <u>Public Safety</u>
	
	 ▪ Animal owners are more likely to comply with public safety measures during an emergency if their animals are also safe. Without detracting from the evacuation and care of humans, a successful response should include the protection of animal populations.
	
	 ▪ Some people may not evacuate if they cannot bring their animals with them.
	
	 ▪ Some people may not shelter-in-place quickly enough if they cannot locate a pet that is outside.
	
	 ▪ Concentrated animal populations may escape during a disaster and endanger people.
	
	    • Many communities have large populations of animals at facilities such as kennels, zoos, and livestock farms.
	
	    • A disaster may destroy buildings or fences that separate animals from the public.
	
	    • Some disasters, such as forest fires, may force wild animals out of their natural habitat and into residential communities or urban areas.
	
	 <u>Federal Law and Policy</u>
	
	 ▪ Pet Evacuation and Transportation Standards (PETS) Act and Post-Katrina Emergency Management Reform Act
	
	    • Mandates state and local communities to incorporate provisions in their emergency plans for people with household pets and service animals
	
	    • Provides FEMA with the authority to set standards for pet plans, to mobilize Federal

Animal Issues in Emergency Management

INSTRUCTOR GUIDANCE	CONTENT
	resources in support of pet response, and to assist states and local communities with the cost of pet response in certain Federally declared disasters
	▪ Homeland Security Presidential Directive (HSPD-9)
	• States that agricultural and food systems are critical infrastructures
	• Directs Federal agencies to protect food and agricultural systems in specific ways
	▪ National Response Framework (NRF)
	• Directs individuals and families to develop emergency plans for their own pets and service animals
	• Gives the local appointed official responsibility for ensuring that local emergency plans account for individuals with service animals and household pets
	• Makes local, tribal, and State jurisdictions responsible for activating a veterinarian/animal response team during an incident
	• Requires the State to consider those with pets or service animals if evacuation is ordered
	• Designates a function that is responsible for supporting and coordinating animal response and relief activities during a Federal response to an incident (Emergency Support Function [ESF] #11 – Agriculture and Natural Resources)
	<u>Public Health</u>
	▪ Some disease or bioterrorism attacks could affect animals in numbers large enough to cause public health concerns for humans or to impact food supplies.
	▪ Some bioterrorism attacks (anthrax, plague, etc.) could infect animals as well as people, and animal cases could spread to people.
	▪ In some disease emergencies, such as a West Nile

Animal Issues in Emergency Management

INSTRUCTOR GUIDANCE	CONTENT
	virus outbreak, the disease may be discovered first in animal populations.

- Zoonotic diseases (diseases that can spread between animals and people) may spread more easily during times of disaster.

  - For example, floodwaters may carry a zoonotic disease such as Salmonella from farm animal manure and affect those who have contact with the water.

Economic Impact

- Animal agriculture is a critical part of our economy.
- If livestock and other animal farms are not protected during a disaster, the interruption of animal agriculture will spread to other aspects of the economy.

  - A large portion of the U.S. economy depends on animal agriculture.

  - Many U.S. jobs are connected to animal agriculture.

  - Interruption of animal agriculture will create a loss in gross domestic product.

Environmental concerns

- Protecting wildlife is essential to maintaining the local natural environment.
- Disaster can cause the spread of biological and toxic contaminants, harming trees and plants and affecting water supplies.

Animal Issues in Emergency Management

INSTRUCTOR GUIDANCE	CONTENT
	<u>Safety of First Responders</u> ▪ First responders may encounter animals during the course of their emergency response duties. ▪ First responders may have direct responsibilities related to the care or management of animals during a disaster. ▪ The safety of first responders requires preparation, knowledge, and equipment to manage and handle animals. Conclude that all of the points mentioned underscore the magnitude of animal issues in the management of a disaster. Animal issues have a widespread effect on local communities and our nation. The issues raised by this discussion will be covered in this session and in *CERT Animal Response II*.

INSTRUCTOR GUIDANCE	CONTENT
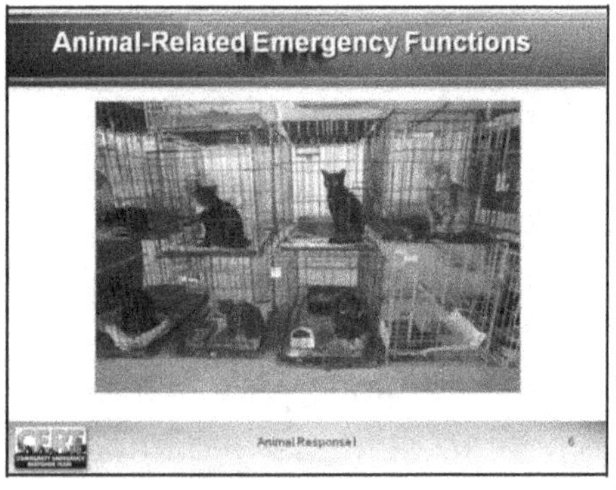**Display Slide 6**  Record responses on an easel pad or white board. Suggested responses: • Needs assessment • Animal populations • Evacuation • Transport • Emergency animal shelters • Search and rescue • Reuniting with owners • Shelter-in-place support • Veterinary care • Animal decontamination • Wildlife populations • Deceased animals • Disease emergencies	***Animal-Related Emergency Management Functions*** Introduce the next topic, "Animal-Related Emergency Management Functions." **What emergency management functions involve animals?**

Animal-Related Emergency Management Functions

INSTRUCTOR GUIDANCE	CONTENT

	Cover any of the following information on animal-related emergency management functions that was not already covered in the class discussion.
	
	Emergency Management Functions Involving Animals:
	- Performing needs assessment
	  - Assessing the effect of disaster on animal facilities, zoos, livestock farms, etc.
	- Managing animal populations
	  - Displaced animals
	  - Animal control
	  - Management of strays
	- Evacuating animals
	  - Household pets
	  - Service animals
	- Transporting animals
	  - Out of the disaster area
	  - Between home and shelters
	- Managing emergency animal shelters
	- Animal search and rescue
	- Reuniting animals and owners
	- Supporting shelters in place
	- Providing veterinary care
	  - Triage and clinical care
	  - Biological risk management (infection control, disease management, animal congregate facilities)
	  - Public health support (e.g., zoonotic disease control during veterinary interaction)
	- Decontaminating animals

Animal-Related Emergency Management Functions

INSTRUCTOR GUIDANCE	CONTENT
	<ul><li>Managing wildlife populations</li><li>Dealing with deceased animals</li><li>Responding to disease emergencies<ul><li>Animal disease</li><li>Zoonotic disease</li></ul></li><li>Carrying out other functions not primarily associated with animal response, e.g., CERTs managing encounters with animals that need assistance when conducting primary CERT activities</li></ul>

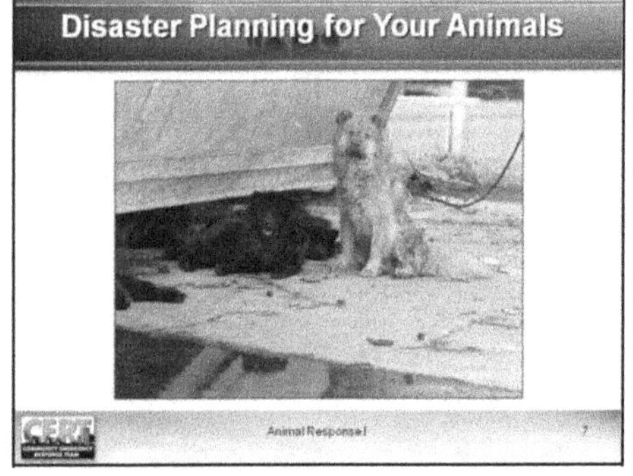

Display Slide 7

No response is required other than a show of hands.

Briefly describe any details of the local jurisdiction's Emergency Operations Plan that address animal issues.

Disaster Planning for Your Animals

Introduce the next topic, "Disaster Planning for Your Animals."

How many of you own animals?

How many of you have family or friends who own animals?

Emphasize that this topic is important to everyone and that CERT members should encourage family and friends to include animals in their preparedness planning.

INSTRUCTOR GUIDANCE	CONTENT
	Recall the Federal law and policies relating to animals in disasters that were mentioned earlier. Note that local jurisdictions, as well as organizations such as local humane societies, should also have plans in place to address animal issues during disasters.

Preparing for a Disaster

Stress the importance of preparing for a disaster.

What are some steps you can take to prepare for a disaster?

Suggested responses:

1. Identify potential hazards

2. Reduce hazards wherever possible

3. Create a disaster plan

4. Develop a disaster supply kit

5. Get training

6. Know your community's disaster response plan

Display Slide 8

Review the information on the slide if it was not already covered in class discussion.

CERTs should prepare for disasters by:

- Identifying potential hazards

- Mitigating hazards

- Creating a disaster plan

- Developing a disaster supply kit

- Participating in training and exercises

- Knowing your community's disaster response plan

Explain that disaster preparedness applies to animals as well as humans. These preparedness steps will be covered next in more detail.

INSTRUCTOR GUIDANCE	CONTENT
 **Display Slide 9**  Suggested responses: Insert information on disasters that are likely to occur locally.  Suggested responses: Insert information about how disasters likely to occur in your area could affect specific animal populations, including household pets and service animals, and livestock and wild animals that may be common in or near your community.	**Identifying Potential Hazards** **What local disasters could occur that might affect animals?** **How could a disaster affect your animals and other animals in your area?**

INSTRUCTOR GUIDANCE	CONTENT
 **Display Slide 10**	**Mitigating Hazards** Cover the following information: Hazard mitigation means taking steps to reduce or eliminate the impact of disasters, such as making changes to protect property and facilities. Some examples of hazard mitigation are: ■ Encouraging animal facilities to relocate out of disaster-prone areas ■ Encouraging animal facilities to retrofit their facilities for hazards in the area (e.g. earthquake straps, hurricane clips) ■ Encouraging livestock owners to maintain adequate insurance against potential loss of livestock and facilities Explain that it is important to reduce potential disaster impact wherever possible, and that animal owners can take their own hazard mitigation steps. Introduce the video, "Animals in Emergencies for Owners." This video, developed by the Chemical Stockpile Emergency Preparedness Program (CSEPP) and FEMA, is intended to help pet and livestock owners prepare to protect their animals during emergencies. Note that the video is 35 minutes long.

Disaster Planning for Your Animals

Disaster Planning for Your Animals

INSTRUCTOR GUIDANCE	CONTENT
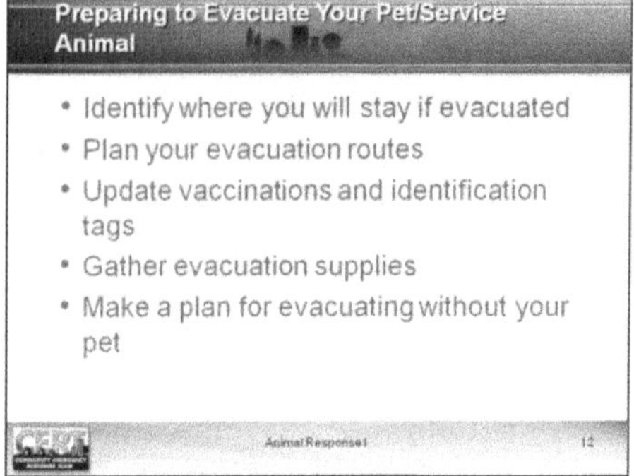 **Display Slide 11**	**Creating a Disaster Plan for Animals** One of the best ways to prepare for a disaster is to create a disaster plan and a disaster supply kit before an emergency occurs. Participants already learned about creating a disaster plan for their families during *CERT Basic Training*. This topic will focus on creating a disaster plan for their animals. Explain that disaster planning for animals includes a number of elements:

- Preparing to evacuate your pet or service animal

- Preparing to stay at home with your pets or service animals during a disaster

- Caring for pets and service animals after a disaster

- Making preparations for livestock

- Taking special considerations for exotic animals

Display Slide 12

Preparing to Evacuate Your Pet or Service Animal

Explain that the following considerations apply to both pets and service animals even though they are distinct categories of animals. Present the following general considerations for preparing to evacuate your pet or service animal:

- There are many reasons to prepare for evacuation:

  - You may have to evacuate at any time – whenever you feel unsafe or are instructed to evacuate by local authorities.

  - It may be unsafe for you to shelter at home during certain disasters.

  - Evacuating with animals takes more time.

  - Preparing in advance will help you evacuate more quickly and give you more options.

- Identify where you will stay.

- Because space for animals in public shelters may be limited, you should find private accommodation for you and your pets if possible.

INSTRUCTOR GUIDANCE	CONTENT
	<ul><li>Make arrangements with family or friends outside your area.</li><li>Find out which motels and hotels in the area to which you intend to evacuate allow pets. Travel guides may contain this information.</li><li>Boarding kennels and veterinary facilities may be able to accommodate your pets during a disaster as well. Find out in advance where pet boarding facilities are located. Be sure to research some outside your local area in case local facilities are at capacity or closed during an emergency.</li><li>Many communities are working to establish emergency pet shelters that are either centrally located (such as at the local animal shelter) or are co-located in proximity to an evacuation shelter for people. Such co-located shelters often require that the owners provide care and exercise for their own pets.</li><li>Most boarding kennels, veterinarians, and animal shelters will need your pet's medical records to make sure all vaccinations are current. Include copies in your pet disaster supply kit along with a photo of your pet.</li><li>Include your local animal control agency, animal shelter, and veterinarian in your list of emergency phone numbers. They may be able to provide information and assistance concerning pets during a disaster.</li></ul>• Plan your evacuation routes.<ul><li>Plan at least two routes to your prearranged location.</li><li>Consider evacuation traffic, fuel availability, distance, and time of day.</li><li>Keep cars and trucks at least half full of gas whenever possible; ensure that gas tanks are full before major storms.</li><li>Remember that a battery-powered radio will be</li></ul>

Disaster Planning for Your Animals

Disaster Planning for Your Animals

INSTRUCTOR GUIDANCE	CONTENT
	the most reliable way to get alerts and news about evacuations during the emergency. ■ Update vaccinations and identification tags. • Make sure vaccinations and medical records are current and be sure to bring copies with you. Many locations will not accept pets without proof of current vaccinations. • Make sure identification tags are up to date and securely fastened to your pet's collar. If possible, attach the address and/or phone number of your evacuation site. If your pet gets lost, its tag is its ticket home. Make sure you have a current photo of your pet for identification purposes. • Another method of pet identification is an I.D. microchip. This tiny device is implanted under the skin and, when scanned, will provide a unique number that can be traced back to your registration information. Consult your veterinarian about I.D. microchips for pets. ■ Gather evacuation supplies: • Having supplies for your pet or service animal already collected in an easy-to-grab kit will make your evacuation faster and easier. • Disaster supply kits for animals will be covered in more detail in a later section. ■ Make a plan for evacuating without your pet. ■ If you have no alternative but to leave your pet at home, there are some precautions you must take, but remember that leaving your pet at home alone can place your animal in great danger. • Plan for confining your pet to a safe area inside. Leave your pet loose inside your home with food and plenty of water. NEVER leave your pet chained outside. • In addition to leaving lots of water, you can raise the lid and seat of the toilet bowl and brace the bathroom door open so your pet can drink. Place

INSTRUCTOR GUIDANCE	CONTENT
	a notice outside in a visible area, advising what types of pets are in the house and where they are located. Provide a phone number where you or a contact can be reached as well as the name and number of your vet.

Display Slide 13

Preparing to Stay at Home with Pets or Service Animals During a Disaster

Present the following information from FEMA on staying at home with pets during a disaster:

- Bring your pets inside immediately.

- Have newspapers on hand for sanitary purposes.

- Remember that animals have instincts about severe weather changes and will often isolate themselves if they are afraid. Bringing them inside early can stop them from running away. Never leave a pet outside or tied up during a storm. If dogs are very afraid of severe weather, confining them to an appropriately sized airline crate may help calm them down and keep them from causing damage.

- Separate dogs and cats. Even if your dogs and cats normally get along, the anxiety of an emergency situation can cause pets to act irrationally.

- Keep smaller pets, such as gerbils and birds, away from cats and dogs.

INSTRUCTOR GUIDANCE	CONTENT

Display Slide 14

Caring for Pets and Service Animals After a Disaster

Present the following information from FEMA on caring for pets and service animals after a disaster:

- The behavior of your pets may change after an emergency. Normally quiet and friendly pets may become fearful, aggressive, or defensive. Watch animals closely.

- In the first few days after the disaster, be prepared to leash your pets when they go outside. Always maintain close contact. Familiar scents and landmarks may be altered, and your pet may become confused and lost.

- Snakes and other wildlife may be displaced and end up in residential or urban areas during and after a disaster. They may pose a threat to pets.

- Downed power lines are another hazard, along with disaster debris.

Display Slide 15

Making Preparations for Livestock

Cover the following information on disaster considerations for livestock:

If you have large animals such as horses, cattle, sheep, goats, or pigs on your property, there are some unique considerations for disaster preparedness:

- Ensure that all animals have some form of identification, e.g., brand, ear tag, or chip, to facilitate their return.

- In flooding or wildfire situations, evacuation may mean moving herds to nearby higher ground or pastures in fire-resistant areas.

- If livestock evacuation requires relocation via truck or trailer, owners need to make advance arrangements for transportation, including routes and destination sheltering sites. Alternate routes should be mapped out in case the planned route is inaccessible.

INSTRUCTOR GUIDANCE	CONTENT
	<ul><li>The sites you evacuate to should have or be able to readily obtain food, water, veterinary care, handling equipment, and facilities.</li><li>If evacuation is not possible, a decision must be made whether to move large animals to available shelter or turn them outside. This decision should be determined based on the type of disaster and the soundness and location of the shelter (structure).</li></ul>Explain the following about the precautions that livestock producers must also take for severe winter weather:<ul><li>When temperatures plunge below zero, livestock need extra attention. Action must be taken to prevent hypothermia, frostbite, and other cold-weather injuries in livestock.</li><li>Make sure your livestock have the following help to prevent cold-weather maladies:<ul><li>Shelter</li><li>Plenty of dry bedding to insulate vulnerable udders, genitals, and legs from the frozen ground and frigid winds</li><li>Windbreaks to keep animals safe from frigid conditions</li><li>Plenty of food and drinkable (not frozen) water</li></ul></li><li>Take extra time to observe livestock, looking for early signs of disease and injury. Severe cold-weather injuries or death primarily occur in the very young or in animals that are already debilitated.<ul><li>Cases of cold weather-related sudden death in calves often result when cattle are suffering from undetected infection, particularly pneumonia.</li><li>Sudden, unexplained livestock deaths and illnesses should be investigated quickly so that a cause can be identified and steps can be taken to protect remaining animals.</li><li>Animals suffering from frostbite don't exhibit pain. It may be up to two weeks before the injury</li></ul></li></ul>

INSTRUCTOR GUIDANCE	CONTENT
	becomes evident as freeze-damaged tissue starts to slough away. At that point, a veterinarian should be consulted.

Display Slide 16

Special Considerations for Exotic Animals

Describe any local policies or regulations that have been adopted regarding exotic animals:

- For large exotic wildlife (lions, large snakes, etc.), owners should have a plan for keeping animals secure during emergencies to avoid release of animals.

- For small exotic pet species (birds, small non-poisonous reptiles, etc.), you may need to provide special environments for sheltering and care. Many of these species need appropriate temperatures, controlled humidity, and low-noise environments. Zoos and veterinary hospitals may be better able to provide the specialized care needed for these pets

- Certain types of exotic animals are difficult to maintain in emergency shelters and may need to be separated due to liability issues.

- Certain types of exotic animals may need to be registered with authorities.

Recommend that participants who own or are otherwise concerned about regulation of exotic pets should consult their State laws and local ordinances.

INSTRUCTOR GUIDANCE	CONTENT

Display Slide 17

Slide content:
Assembling a Disaster Supply Kit
- Evacuation Checklist
  - For pets/service animals
  - For livestock
- Shelter-in-Place Checklist
  - For pets/service animals
  - For livestock
- Post information for emergency personnel on your property

Assembling a Disaster Supply Kit for Animals

As an important part of disaster planning, explain that a disaster supply kit should include an evacuation or "go kit" that will sustain their animals for 72 hours and stay-at-home supplies that will sustain their animals for up to two weeks.

Stress that it is also very important to post contact and animal information on the property when the owner has evacuated without their animal(s). This will assist emergency personnel who arrive on the scene.

Details of information to be provided are included in the Disaster Supply Checklists below.

Have participants review the Disaster Supply Checklists on the following pages.

Evacuation Checklist for Pets and Service Animals

☐ Carriers/airline kennels (one per animal)
 Note: pillowcases may be used to transport cats in emergencies
☐ Collars (with tags), leashes, harnesses, muzzles
☐ Registration papers, vaccination records, veterinarian's contact information
☐ Bowls (food dishes and larger water dishes or dispensers)
☐ Blankets or bedding
☐ Paper towels, spray cleaner, trash bags
☐ Litter box, litter
☐ Medications, first aid kit
☐ Water for three days
☐ Dry food, canned food for three days
☐ Treats and toys

Disaster Planning for Your Animals

INSTRUCTOR GUIDANCE	CONTENT
	Stay-at-Home Checklist for Pets and Service Animals ☐ Flashlights or lantern, extra batteries ☐ For aquariums, battery-operated air pump with extra batteries ☐ Medications ☐ Snow shovel, snow shoes, cold-weather gear where appropriate ☐ Pet food for two weeks ☐ Stored water for two weeks
If your area is prone to heat emergencies, emphasize the need for owners to provide for adequate hydration for livestock during these events.	**Evacuation Checklist for Livestock** ☐ Halters and lead ropes ☐ Registration, brand inspection papers, veterinarian's contact information, and medical records ☐ Saddles, pads, bridles, hoof pick, hoof knives, rasp, brushes, rope, lunge line ☐ Water buckets, grain pans ☐ Medications, first aid kit ☐ Water source ☐ Hay and grain **Stay-at-Home Checklist for Livestock** ☐ Flashlights or lantern, extra batteries ☐ Camp stove and 2 or more gallons fuel for melting ice or snow for water or a generator and fuel to power a well ☐ Medications ☐ Winter gear (boots, coats, coveralls, gloves) where appropriate ☐ Maintain 1-2 weeks supply of hay/grain at all times ☐ Water for 1-2 weeks (include considerations for extreme heat)

INSTRUCTOR GUIDANCE	CONTENT

Information to Post for Emergency Personnel on Your Property if You Are Leaving Your Pets or Livestock Behind

☐ Your contact information (daytime/cell phone number, other emergency contacts)
☐ Vet contact information
☐ Number of pets (including location, basic description, and name[s])
☐ Number of livestock (including location and basic description)
☐ Location of animal emergency supplies
☐ Permission for emergency personnel to evacuate your animal(s) in your absence

Exercise: Design a Disaster Plan

Purpose: This exercise allows participants to leave the class with a concrete plan for preparing their own animals for a disaster.

Instructions: Follow the steps below to conduct the exercise.

1. Refer participants back to the disaster planning guidance and emergency supply checklists reviewed earlier in this topic.

2. Instruct participants to individually write out a disaster plan for their animals or animals they know. Tell them to be sure to note any elements in the plan that require more information.

3. Remind participants that their plan should include:

   - Shelter options

   - Evacuation supplies (for 72 hours)

   - Shelter-in-place supplies (for 1-2 weeks)

   - Emergency contact information

   - Description of animals

4. Allow 20 minutes for participants to complete their

INSTRUCTOR GUIDANCE	CONTENT
	plans.
	5. Ask if anyone has a livestock farm, and have that person share his or her list with the rest of the class.
	6. Ask if anyone has an exotic pet, and have that person share his or her list with the rest of the class.
	7. Ask if anyone has a (insert type of animal that is common in the local area), and have that person share his or her list with the rest of the class.
	Debrief: Congratulate participants for beginning the process of preparing their animals for a disaster. Encourage them to follow through by researching any missing details, making the preparations outlined in their plans, and gathering emergency animal supplies that can be placed with their family disaster kits.

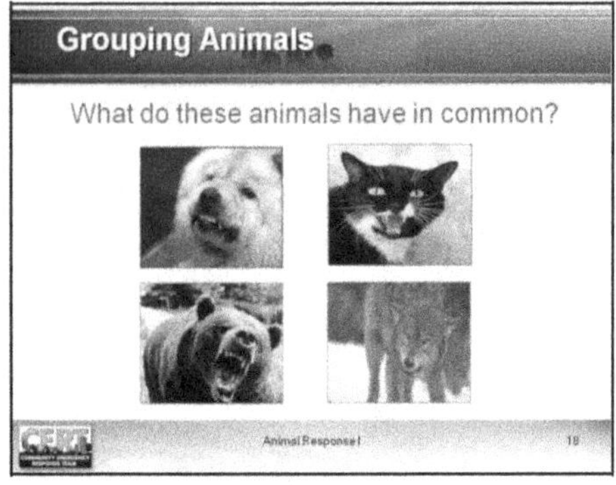

Display Slide 18

Suggested response: They are all predators.

General Animal Behavior

Introduce the next topic, "General Animal Behavior."

Grouping Animals

What do all of the animals pictured on this slide have in common?

INSTRUCTOR GUIDANCE	CONTENT

Display Slide 19	**Characteristics of Predator Animals**
	
	Describe the following common characteristics of predator animals:
	
	- Vision
	  - Binocular
	  - Excellent depth perception
	  - Eyes facing forward
	- Feet
	  - Claws or nails
	- Teeth
	  - Built for penetration, biting, tearing
	- Instincts
	  - Hunt
	  - Chase
	  - Kill
	
	What are some examples of predator animals?

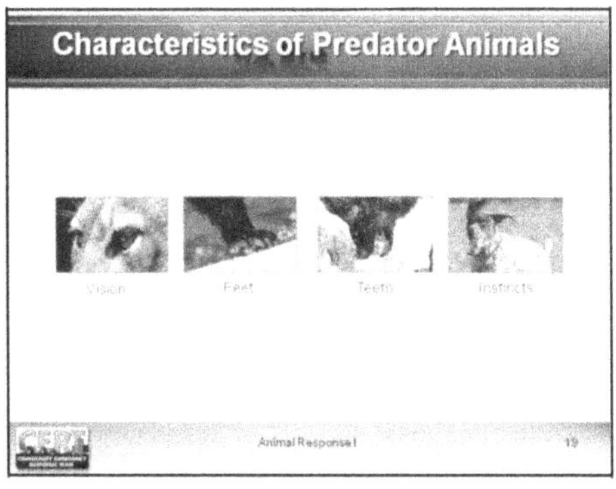

Suggested Responses:

- Cats
- Dogs
- Bears
- Wolves
- Foxes
- Birds of prey

General Animal Behavior

INSTRUCTOR GUIDANCE	CONTENT

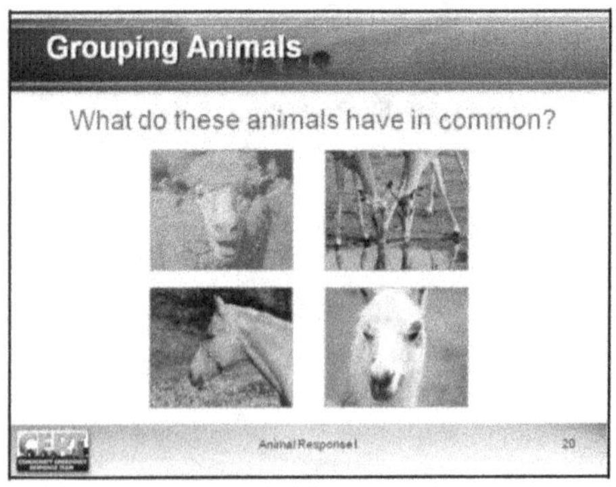

Display Slide 20

Suggested response: They are all prey animals.

What do the animals on this slide have in common?

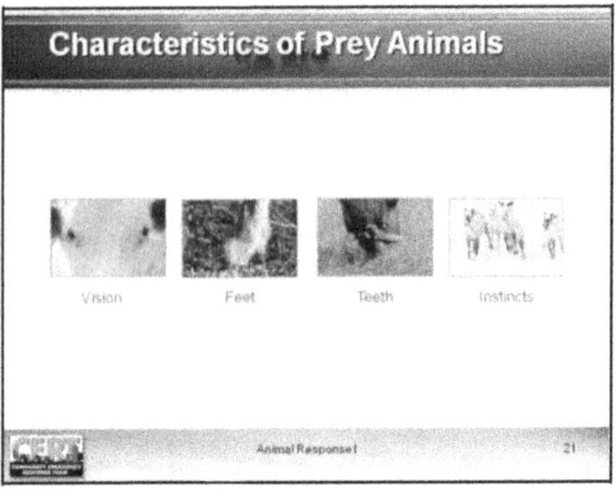

Display Slide 21

Characteristics of Prey Animals

Describe the following common characteristics of prey animals:

- Vision
  - Wide field of vision
  - Eyes typically face to the side
- Feet
  - Hooves for running and pawing
- Teeth
  - Built for grazing, grinding
- Instincts
  - Escape
  - Run

INSTRUCTOR GUIDANCE	CONTENT
 Suggested Responses: - Goats - Sheep - Alpacas - Cows - Deer - Horses	**What are some examples of prey animals?**

Animal Domestication

Cover the following information:

- Animal domestication means breeding species for desired physical and behavioral characteristics. Animals are usually bred for characteristics that increase food and milk production or work and service abilities or for companion traits.

- Domesticated animals often exhibit compliance, trust in people, and a calm, non-aggressive demeanor.

- Domesticated animals may revert to instinctive behavior during stressful situations. Predator animals may revert to chasing and attacking, while prey animals may run or hide. Domesticated predator animals such as dogs may even attack prey animals such as livestock if fences have been torn down and there is nothing to separate the animals.

- Responders should be mindful of instinctive predator and prey behaviors when trying to herd, handle, or manage animals during emergency situations.

Display Slide 22

General Animal Behavior

<table>
<tr><th>INSTRUCTOR GUIDANCE</th><th>CONTENT</th></tr>
</table>

Species Specific Behavior and Body Language

<u>Exercise: Dog and Cat Behavior</u>

Tell participants that dogs and cats are very common domestic animals. They provide good examples of what to watch for in animal behavior under stressful circumstances.

Introduce the following exercise by telling participants that they will now work in teams to test their knowledge of animal behavior and share information.

<u>Purpose:</u> This exercise allows participants to test their knowledge of animal behavior and share information with each other.

<u>Instructions:</u> Follow the steps below to conduct the exercise.

1. Divide the class into two teams and give each team a bell.

2. Ask participants to close their Participant Manuals for the game and let them open them after the game to write down answers as you review them.

3. Explain the rules of the game:

   - After you ask each question, you will call on whichever team rings the bell first.

   - The participant who rings the bell first gets to answer the question. If the participant answers correctly, his or her team receives 100 points.

   - If the participant answers incorrectly, another participant from the same team can try to answer the same question. If the second participant answers correctly, you will give his or her team 100 points.

   - If he or she answers incorrectly, you will subtract 50 points from the team's score and provide the correct answer or answers. (Make sure you cover all of the answers listed on the left.)

INSTRUCTOR GUIDANCE	CONTENT
	4. Ask each question listed below. Keep track of each team's score on your easel pad or white board. 5. Pass out a bag of candy or candy bars (or animal crackers) to the winning team.
Answers to questions:	<u>Game Questions:</u>
1. Any three of the following: Territorial, protective, frightened, physical pain, aggression/dominance issues	1. A dog may bite if it is feeling________? (Name three reasons.)
2. Any three of the following: Submissive, friendly, fearful, threatening, aggressive, ambivalent, escape behavior	2. A dog confronted by a stranger may react in what ways? (Name three.)
3. Mood or behavior	3. You can use a dog's facial expressions, body language, and vocalizations to predict its_________.
4. Any one of the following: ear position, mouth position, gaze direction, gaze intensity	4. You can read a dog's facial expression by paying attention to the dog's .
5. True	5. True or false: The best way to meet a dog is to ignore it and let it approach you.
6. With your side to the dog	6. If you do approach a new dog, how should you position your body?

General Animal Behavior

INSTRUCTOR GUIDANCE	CONTENT
7. They are warning signs.	7. What do these dog expressions have in common? Ears pinned to head, ears forward and stiff, tail straight up, tail tucked under body, direct stare, showing whites of the eyes, licking lips, yawning, body tension, and end of tail-wagging?
8. Loud voice, standing over, bending over, prolonged eye contact, sudden movement	8. What types of body language should you avoid when dealing with an unknown dog? List three.
9. True	9. True or false: The proper behavior for approaching and controlling an unknown dog is to use a soft voice, look 45 degrees to the left or right of the dog and avoid meeting the dog's eyes, move slowly, and squat down.
10. Cat	10. Does the following behavior describe a cat or a dog? Prefers privacy, is quick to defend itself, will not normally approach strangers, needs time to feel comfortable in a new environment.
11. False	11. True or false: Cats and dogs are behaviorally similar.
12. Growling or hissing	12. What kind of vocalization might you hear from an aggressive cat?
13. Any two of the following: lowering head, holding ears to back or side of head, arching back, fluffing tail and holding it erect	13. What are other signs of aggression in a cat? (List two.)
14. Fear	14. Crouching low to ground, fluffing hair along back, pulling tail to the side, dilating pupils, and flattening ears all signal what behavioral state in a cat?

General Animal Behavior

INSTRUCTOR GUIDANCE	CONTENT
15. Dog	15. Is it normally easier to read the behavior of a dog or a cat?
16. Escape	16. A cat that feels threatened may climb anything, even people and walls, to________.

<u>Debrief:</u> Review all of the answers to the game and let participants write their answers into their Participant Manuals.

Conclude the exercise by telling participants that recognizing the facial expressions and body language of dogs and cats will prepare them for handling these animals correctly during emergency response.

Explain that the next section will cover animal behavior and body language in more detail.

Dog Facial Expressions

Review the facial expressions on the slide, adding comments as appropriate.

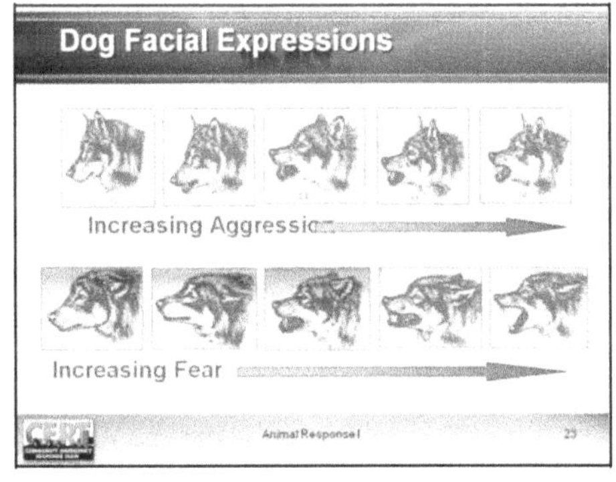

Display Slide 23

INSTRUCTOR GUIDANCE	CONTENT

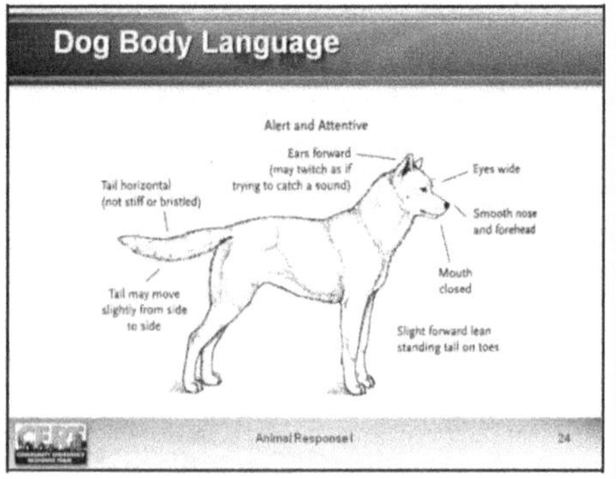

Display Slide 24

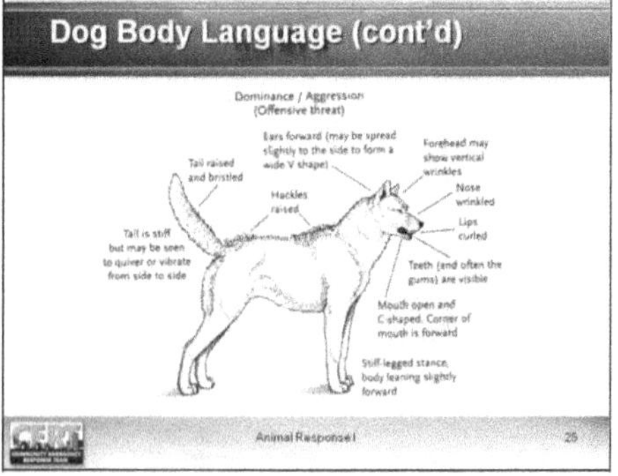

Display Slide 25

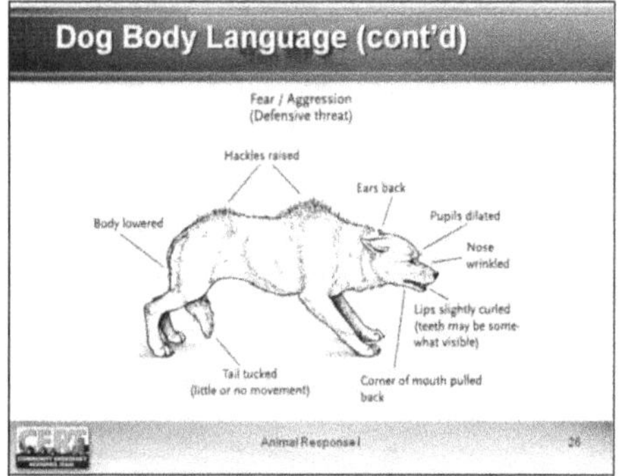

Display Slide 26

Dog Body Language

Review the body language of the dogs pictured on slides 24 to 29, making sure you point out the characteristics described on each slide.

INSTRUCTOR GUIDANCE	CONTENT
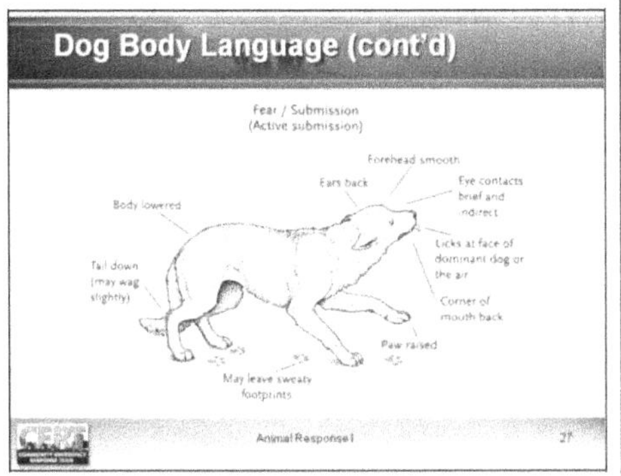 **Display Slide 27** 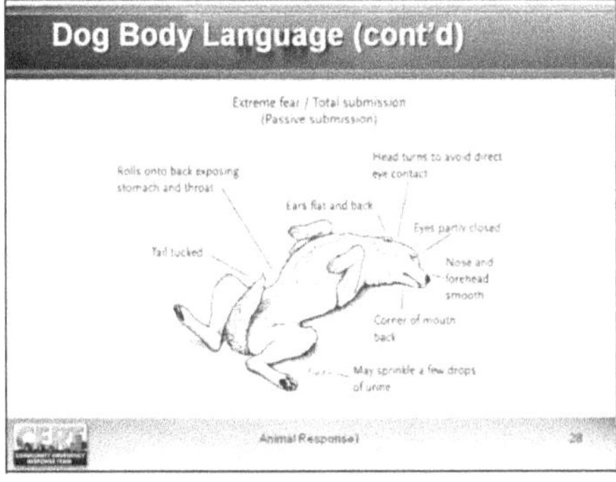 **Display Slide 28**	

INSTRUCTOR GUIDANCE	CONTENT
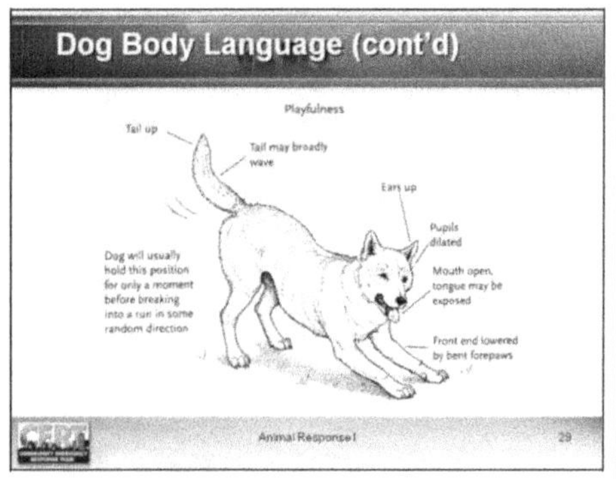 **Display Slide 29**	
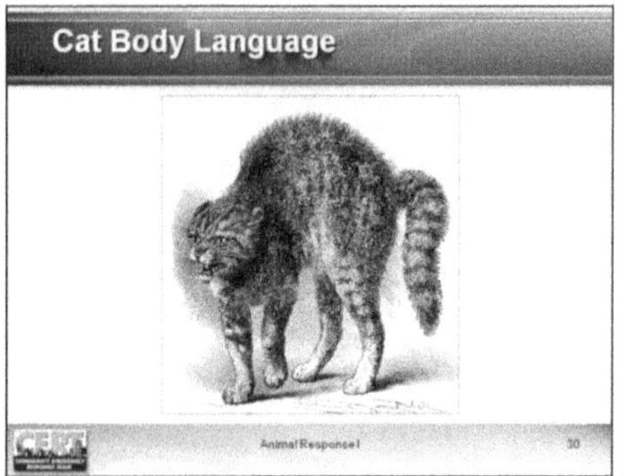 **Display Slide 30**	**Cat Body Language** Have participants look at the slide. Point out the following characteristics of an aggressive cat: - Standing with rear higher than front - Tail down - Ears out to side of head - Direct eye contact - Raised hair on back
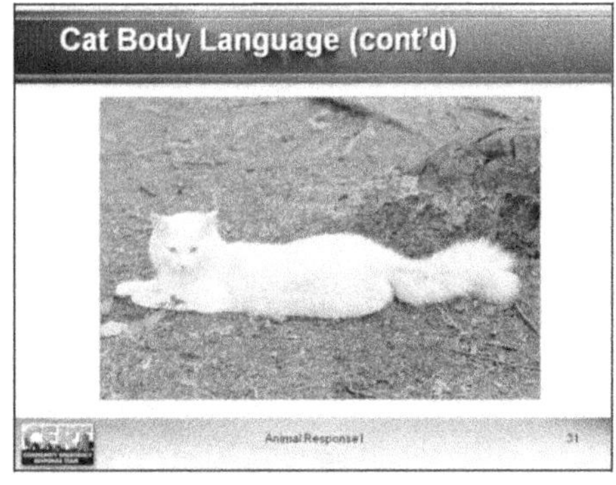 **Display Slide 31**	Have participants look at the slide. Point out the following characteristics of a relaxed cat: - Relaxed posture - Relaxed tail - Ears pointing up and out - Claws retracted

INSTRUCTOR GUIDANCE	CONTENT

Display Slide 32	**Horses, Cattle, and Swine**
	
	Cover the following information:
	
	Horses
	
	■ Instincts
	  • Herd animals
	  • Prey animals
	  • Fear the unknown
	  • Run away when frightened
	  • Use hooves and teeth for protection
	
	■ Senses
	  • Have excellent hearing and vision, though close vision in front of the face is limited
	  • Have an excellent sense of smell, which may cause heightened fear of smoke and fire
	  • Can hear in all directions
	  • Are sensitive to human moods and attitudes and can sense fear or agitation in others
	  • Are sensitive to atmospheric changes
	
	■ Behavior
	  • Horses should always be kept calm.
	  • Even a small horse or a pony can overpower an adult when frightened.
	  • Most horses trust humans and see them as the dominant animal of the herd.
	  • Horses will generally cooperate when approached calmly and quietly.
	  • Horses become more flighty in windy weather.
	
	■ Body Language
	  • Ears: Mobile, expressive, move independently, point toward items of interest
	    • If ears are pointed back, this could mean the horse feels angry or aggressive or is listening

INSTRUCTOR GUIDANCE	CONTENT

	to sounds from behind.
	
	• If ears are pointed back and out, the horse may be bored.
	
	• Ears pointing forward indicate interest. If interest is directed toward another horse, you may need to control or deflect the encounter.
	
	• Ears flat to the neck are a warning sign: Watch out!
	
	• Body
	
	  • Raised head or tail may be invitation to play.
	
	  • Head-shaking and tail-swishing may indicate aggression or annoyance, or the horse may be trying to rid itself of flies.
	
	• Head
	
	  • A high head indicates that the horse is about to take action; the horse may be stressed or curious.
	
	  • A stiff, lowered head may mean the horse is stressed or has fallen asleep.
	
	• Legs: An un-weighted hoof may mean the horse is relaxed or cocked and ready to use that hoof. Look at other stress indicators to decide.
	
	• Understanding horse body language requires practical, hands-on experience.
	
	Cattle
	
	▪ Bovids
	
	  • Cattle have an established pecking order.
	
	  • Dominant females and larger, heavier males protect the rest of the herd.
	
	  • Cows have a strong maternal instinct.
	
	▪ Bulls
	
	  • Bulls are more aggressive during mating season.
	
	  • Dairy bulls are more aggressive than beef bulls

INSTRUCTOR GUIDANCE	CONTENT

	and may be extremely dangerous.
	
	- Never try to manage a bull alone.
	- Tips
	   • Cattle have minds of their own and may not be easy to lead or herd.
	   • Cattle have a huge weight advantage.
	   • Cattle can move faster than you would expect.
	   • Managing cattle safely requires practice and skill.
	
	Swine
	
	- Pigs come in all sizes and can be very large. Large boars can weigh over 1,000 lbs, and large sows can weigh up to 700 lbs.
	- Large pigs can be dangerous and can inflict severe bite wounds.
	- Pigs cannot be led.
	- Smaller pigs may be put in a cage or a kennel.
	- Pigs must get wet or roll in mud to stay cool.
	
	Let the class know that animal handling, transportation, and herding will be covered in *CERT Animal Response II*.

General Animal Behavior

INSTRUCTOR GUIDANCE	CONTENT

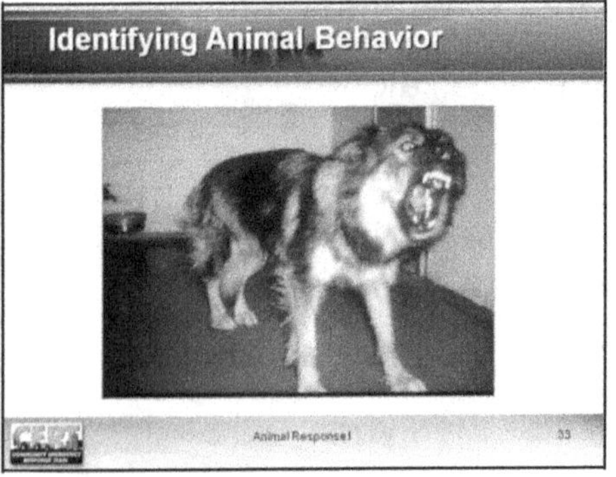

DISPLAY SLIDE 33: Aggressive

Identifying Animal Behavior

Ask participants to identify the behavior of the animals presented on slides 33 through 39.

Conclude this section by asking the participants if anyone has questions about animal behavior and body language.

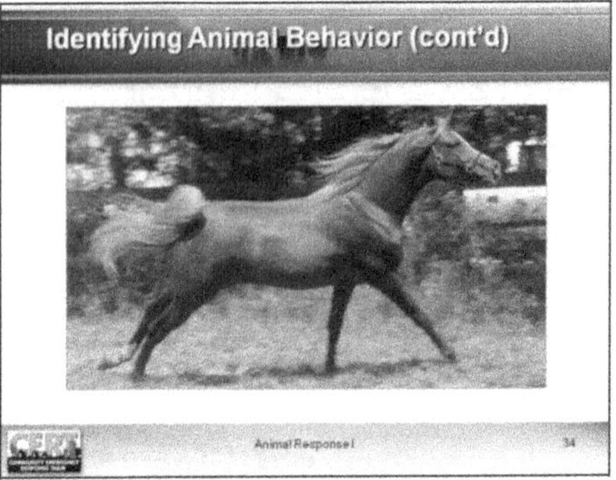

Display Slide 34: Frightened

INSTRUCTOR GUIDANCE	CONTENT
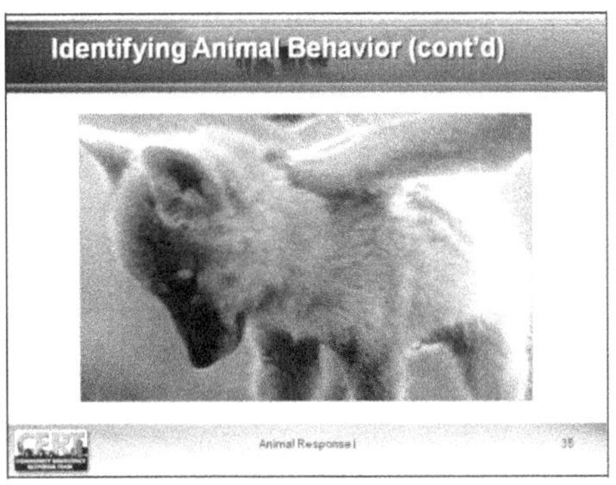 **Display Slide 35:** Submissive 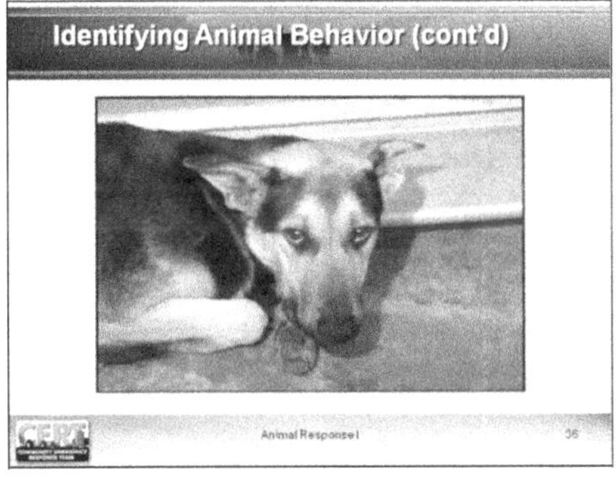 **Display Slide 36:** Frightened 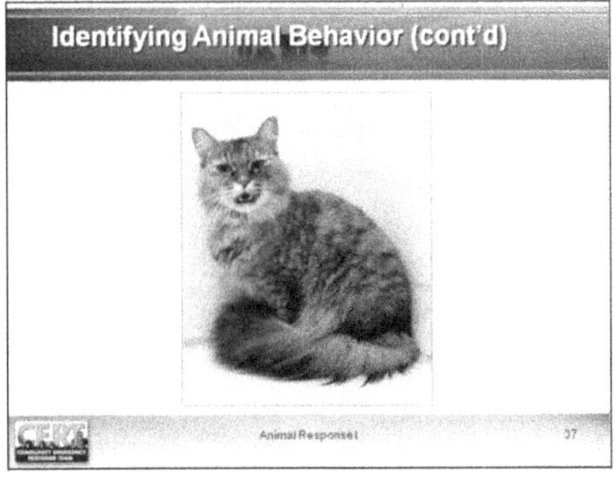 **Display Slide 37:** Aggressive	

General Animal Behavior

INSTRUCTOR GUIDANCE	CONTENT

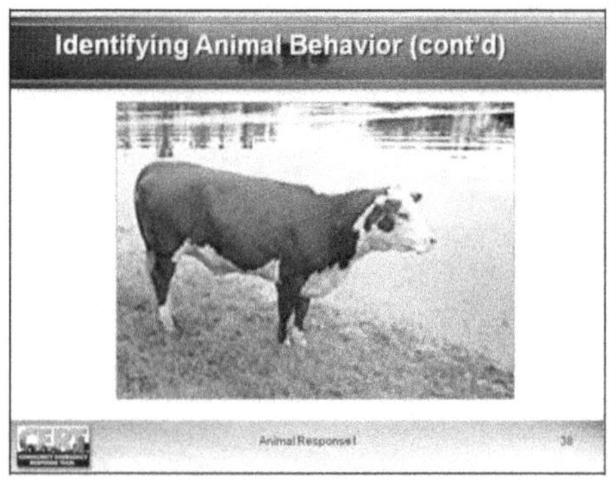

Display Slide 38: Passive

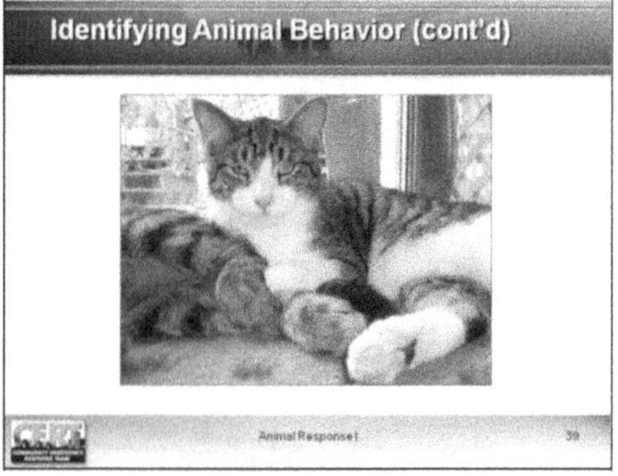

Display Slide 39: Content

INSTRUCTOR GUIDANCE	CONTENT

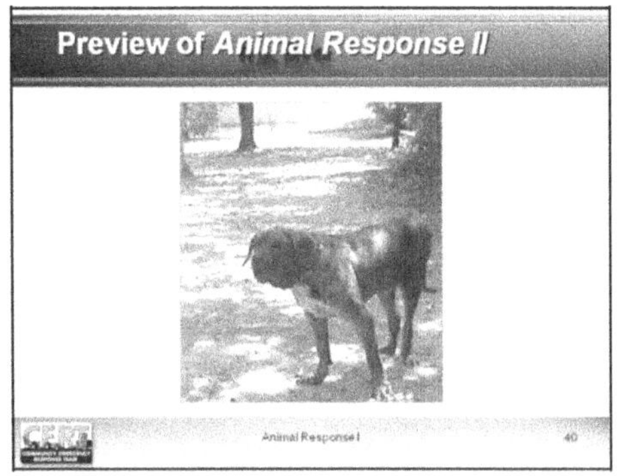

Display Slide 40

Insert local disaster.

Preview of CERT Animal Response II

Scenario

Explain to participants that *CERT Animal Response II* will cover safety of CERT members who encounter animals during the course of their emergency duties.

Ask if they would know what to do in the following situation, and then present the following scenario: An evacuation has been ordered in your community due to an expected (insert local disaster). Your CERT is in contact with local police, and you have been directed to assist an elderly man who refuses to leave his home unless he can take his animal with him. As you begin to approach the house, you are confronted by a large dog. As a trained CERT member and a caring citizen, what can you do?

Emphasize that participants should come back for *CERT Animal Response II* to learn about their role as a CERT member encountering emergency issues involving animals.

Display Slide 41

Topics Covered in *CERT Animal Response II*

Give the participants a preview of *CERT Animal Response II* by briefly mentioning the topics that will be covered in that session:

- Your role as a CERT member responding to issues involving animals

- Protecting your own safety when dealing with animals, including:

  - General response when encountering animals

  - Avoiding transmission of zoonotic disease

  - Basic care for injuries involving animals

- Knowledge and skills you'll need for CERT functions involving animals, including:

  - Cleaning and disinfection

  - General animal care

<table>
<tr><th>INSTRUCTOR GUIDANCE</th><th>CONTENT</th></tr>
<tr><td></td><td>

- Basic animal handling
- Dealing with injured animals
  Communicating with animal owners and caretakers
- Animal identification and tracking

</td></tr>
</table>

Display Slide 42

Module Summary

Summarize the topics that were discussed in this module.

Animal Issues in Emergency Management

Animals are a significant component of disaster preparedness and emergency response. The management of disasters must include a plan for issues affecting animals.

Animal-Related Emergency Management Functions

Animal issues will need to be addressed in almost every emergency management function. During the course of your responsibilities as a CERT volunteer, you may be asked to assist in animal-related tasks. You may also encounter animals while performing other emergency duties.

Disaster Planning for Your Animals

You have now started to develop a disaster plan and an emergency supply checklist to take home with you. Start assembling your animal disaster kit as soon as you can, and place it with your family emergency kit.

General Animal Behavior

Disaster response may include numerous animal-related tasks. You can protect yourself when handling or managing the care of animals by preparing in advance for animal encounters.

INSTRUCTOR GUIDANCE	CONTENT
	### *Closing* **Ask if anyone has any final questions.** Thank participants for attending the session. Tell them the time and location of the *CERT Animal Response II* session and any other upcoming training or CERT program events.

Notes

Notes

Notes

Notes

Notes